In the Footsteps of Explorers

Christopher Columbus

Sailing to a New World

Adrianna Morganelli

Crabtree Publishing Company

www.crabtreebooks.com

Crabtree Publishing Company

www.crabtreebooks.com

For Fred -
and our own future adventure

Coordinating editor: Ellen Rodger
Series editor: Carrie Gleason
Editor: Rachel Eagen
Design and production coordinator: Rosie Gowsell
Cover design and production assistance: Samara Parent
Art direction: Rob MacGregor
Scanning technician: Arlene Arch-Wilson
Photo research: Allison Napier
Consultant: Tracey L.Neikirk, Museum Educator, The Mariners' Museum, Newport News, Virginia

Photo Credits: Private Collection, Archive Charmet;/Bridgeman Art Library: p. 7; The Art Archive/ Bibliotheque Nationale Paris: p. 8; Bettmann/ CORBIS: p. 16; Bibliotheque National, Paris, France, Archives Charmet;/Bridgeman Art Library: p. 4; Library of Congress, Washington D.C., USA,; Bridgeman Art Library: p. 25; Private Collection, Michael Graham-Stewart;/Bridgeman Art Library: pp. 22-23; North Wind/ North Wind Picture Archives: p. 6, pp. 12-13, pp. 14-15, p. 20, p. 21, p. 24, p. 27; Reuters/ CORBIS: p. 31; Scala/ Art Resource, NY: p. 26; Snark/ Art Resource, NY: p. 9, pp. 28-29; Patrick Ward/ CORBIS: p. 30; Other images from stock photo cd

Illustrations: Lauren Fast: p. 4, p. 28; Roman Goforth: p. 27; David Wysotski, Allure Illustrations: pp. 16-17

Cartography: Jim Chernishenko: title page, p. 10

Cover: Columbus leaves Palos, Spain, on his first voyage to the New World.

Title page: Columbus traveled from Spain to the Caribbean.

Sidebar icon: An illustration of Columbus' ship taken from an old map.

Crabtree Publishing Company

www.crabtreebooks.com   1-800-387-7650

Copyright © 2005 CRABTREE PUBLISHING COMPANY.

Cataloging-in-Publication Data
Morganelli, Adrianna, 1979-
    Christopher Columbus : sailing to a new world / Adrianna Morganelli.
(In the footsteps of explorers)
Includes index.
ISBN-13: 978-0-7787-2409-4 (rlb)
ISBN-10: 0-7787-2409-3 (rlb)
ISBN-13: 978-0-7787-2445-2 (pbk)
ISBN-10: 0-7787-2445-X (pbk)
    1. Columbus, Christopher, ca. 1451-1506--Juvenile literature. 2. Explorers--America--Biography--Juvenile literature. 3. Explorers--Spain--Biography--Juvenile literature. 4. America--Discovery and exploration--Spanish--Juvenile literature.
I. Title. II. Series.
E118.M77 2005   j970.01'5'092
                                        C2005-900409-6
                                        LC

Published in the United States
PMB 16A
350 Fifth Ave.
Suite 3308
New York, NY
10118

Published in Canada
616 Welland Ave.
St. Catharines
Ontario, Canada
L2M 5V6

Published in the United Kingdom
73 Lime Walk
Headington
Oxford
OX3 7AD
United Kingdom

Published in Australia
386 Mt. Alexander Rd.
Ascot Vale (Melbourne)
V1C 3032

Contents

A Spirited Sailor 4

Medieval Europe 6

The Early Years 8

Columbus in America 10

Life at Sea 14

Other Voyages 18

Failed Colonies 20

Native Life 22

European Contact 24

After Columbus 26

Columbus' Legacy 30

Glossary and Index 32

A Spirited Sailor

Christopher Columbus was an Italian explorer whose dream was to sail west across the Atlantic Ocean to Asia to trade for spices, gold, and silk. During his travels, he accidentally stumbled upon America, which he believed was Asia.

A Historic Meeting

Columbus' arrival in the New World introduced Europe to America and its peoples, and brought great wealth and power to Spain and other European countries. Europeans called the land the "New World," because for them, the land brought new opportunity. For the people already living there, native groups such as the Taino and the Carib, the Europeans brought new hardships. Columbus' voyages established contact between these two groups of people, which drastically changed life in both Europe and the Americas.

From the Beginning

Christopher Columbus was thought to have been born in Genoa, a city in what is now Italy. Columbus' father, Domenico Colombo, was a wool merchant, and his mother, Susanna Colombo, a wool weaver's daughter. Columbus had little schooling as a child, and did not learn to read or write until he traveled to Portugal many years later. In his youth he worked with his brothers and sister as a **wool carder**. As a young man, Columbus quit the wool trade to become a sailor. Some historians think Columbus was really from Catalonia, in present-day Spain, but they are still gathering evidence for this.

(above) Christopher Columbus was named for Saint Christopher, the patron saint, or protector, of all who travel by land, sea, and air.

In the Words of...

Columbus made four voyages to the New World. On his first voyage, he and his restless crew spotted land after 37 days at sea. When they reached a small island in the **Bahamas**, Columbus claimed it for Spain. When the crew landed, they wept and kissed the earth. Columbus' journal entry describes the Taino, the native peoples who lived on the island:

" *It appeared to me to be a race of people very poor in everything. They go as naked as when their mothers bore them, and so do the women, although I did not see more than one young girl. All I saw were youths, none more than thirty years of age. They are very well made, with very handsome bodies, and very good countenances. Their hair is short and coarse, almost like the hairs of a horse's tail. They wear the hairs brought down to the eyebrows, except a few locks behind, which they wear long and never cut.*"

(right) European artists from the 1500s painted the Taino people without ever having met them.

- 1451 -
Christopher Columbus born in Genoa, Italy.

- October 12, 1492 -
Columbus lands in the Bahamas.

- May 20, 1506 - **Columbus dies in Valladolid, Spain.**

Medieval Europe

Columbus' voyages mark the end of the Middle Ages in Europe. The Middle Ages was a period in history in which exploration was difficult and Europeans did not know much of the world beyond their own borders.

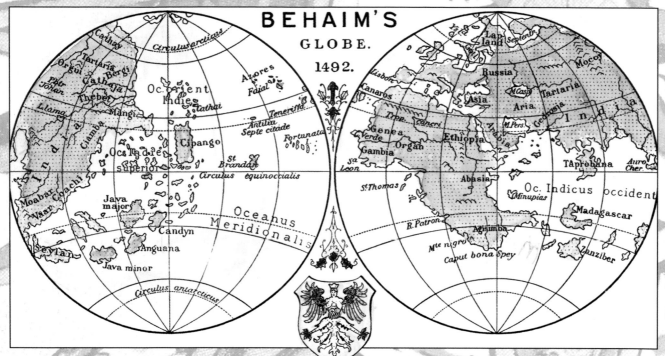

Fabled Lands

In medieval Europe, valuable spices, such as cinnamon, cloves, pepper, and nutmeg, were brought from Asia overland on long **trade routes**. The spices were used to make medicines and hide the taste of salted meat. Asia, or the Indies, was made up of the modern-day countries of India, Burma, China, Japan, Moluccas, and Indonesia. Europeans believed that roads in these lands were paved in gold and gemstones, and that strange and wonderful creatures lived there.

Portuguese Dominance

Portugal was the leading country for sea exploration and discovery. Portugal's prince, Henry the Navigator, learned of the riches of Africa, and studied the geography and trade of that continent. He established the first school in Europe for navigators in Portugal and trained people in **navigation**, mapmaking, and science. Henry **sponsored** many voyages along the western coast of Africa to search for a trade route that would lead to the riches of Asia.

(above) In 1492, Martin Behaim made the first globe, which he called "The Earth Apple."

(left) During the 1400s, European sailors stayed close to the coasts because legends said that the water boiled near the equator and sea monsters swallowed ships.

Columbus' Influence

In 1474, a scientist from Italy named Paolo Toscanelli drew a world map which showed a path from Europe to China. Toscanelli incorrectly calculated that Japan lay 2,700 miles (4345 km) west of Spain. It was pure coincidence that North America happened to be located where he thought Japan was. This geographical information was supplied to the Portuguese king, and Columbus is believed to have read it while in Portugal.

World Views

Around 150 A.D., Greek astronomer and geographer **Claudius Ptolemy** wrote a book called *Geographia*, which included a map of the world. The map showed Asia, Europe, and Africa, which were the only known continents. In the 1400s, Ptolemy's book was translated into Latin and read by many European explorers. According to Ptolemy, there was only one ocean that surrounded all the continents.

- 1271 -
Venetian explorer Marco Polo travels to China, which he calls Cathay, bringing back tales of great wealth.

- 1486 -
Portuguese explorer Bartolomeu Diaz rounds the southernmost tip of Africa, called the Cape of Good Hope.

- 1497 -
Portuguese explorer Vasco da Gama sets out on a voyage that ends with his reaching Asia by sailing around the tip of Africa.

The Early Years

Columbus studied science and geography books and spoke with Portuguese sailors to help him develop a navigation plan. He wanted to find a westward route to Asia across the mysterious waters of the Atlantic.

Bechalla

When Columbus was 25 years old, he sailed aboard the ship *Bechalla* that was carrying **mastic** to be traded at ports in Northern Europe. Off the coast of Portugal, the *Bechalla* was attacked by ships looking to steal the cargo, and after a long battle, the *Bechalla* sank. Columbus survived by swimming to a small fishing harbor in Portugal.

Columbus' Proposal

Columbus believed that the route around Africa was the difficult way to reach Asia, and that sailing west across the Atlantic would take less time. In 1484, Columbus proposed his idea to King John II of Portugal. Columbus explained to the court that if the king sponsored his trip, then Portugal would control the wealth of Asia. The king considered Columbus' proposal for one year, but turned it down because he did not believe that a shorter route across the Atlantic existed.

(below) Columbus worked as a mapmaker in Portugal, drawing maps of the African coast using information given by the Portuguese who controlled the pepper trade route.

Taking a Chance on Spain

Columbus sailed to Spain to appeal to the Spanish king and queen for support. He waited six years for a decision. When Columbus approached King Ferdinand and Queen Isabella in 1486, the country today called Spain did not exist. Ferdinand and Isabella were the rulers of the powerful kingdoms of Aragon and Castile. They sought to bring other territories under Spanish control.

Ferdinand and Isabella were involved in a fierce fight to drive the Moors from Spain. The Moors were **Muslims** who came from North Africa in 711 A.D. In 1492, Ferdinand and Isabella captured the last Moor stronghold and drove them out of the country. That same year, they agreed to sponsor Columbus' voyage. Discovering a new trade route to Asia would increase the king and queen's wealth and grant their country ownership of new lands. Ferdinand and Isabella promised Columbus that he could govern, or rule, lands he found on his route, as well as keep ten percent of all the treasures he found.

(above) With the battle over the Moors won, Ferdinand and Isabella turned their attentions toward gaining wealth through exploration.

Columbus in America

Columbus' crew sailed three ships, the *Nina, Pinta,* and *Santa Maria* from the Spanish port of Palos. They headed for the island of Cipangu, the name Europeans gave to Japan. Columbus believed that beyond Japan, they would reach the Asian mainland of China.

Across the Ocean

Carried by the **trade winds**, Columbus' fleet headed across the Atlantic. After almost a month, the trade winds died down, and calm waters slowed the ships. The crew became restless and began to doubt Columbus' skill as a navigator, or guide. To reassure the crew and avoid **mutiny**, Columbus promised 10,000 gold coins, called *maravedis*, to the first man to spot land. During their four weeks at sea, many members of the crew imagined that they saw land in the distance, and even mistook cloud formations for distant beaches. Crew members looked for signs that land was near, such as flocks of birds flying overhead, and bits of wood and plants floating on the water.

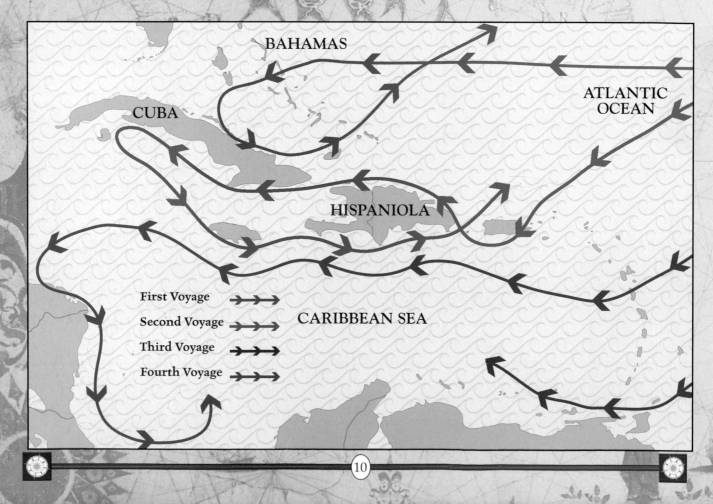

BAHAMAS

CUBA

ATLANTIC OCEAN

HISPANIOLA

First Voyage
Second Voyage
Third Voyage
Fourth Voyage

CARIBBEAN SEA

Tierra! Tierra! (Land! Land!)

Finally, Rodrigo de Triana, the lookout on the *Pinta*, sighted land. The captain of the *Pinta*, Martin Alonso Pinzon, fired a cannon to alert the other ships. Everyone, including Columbus, believed they had reached Asia, but they had actually landed on a small island of the Bahamas chain.

The Quest for Gold

Columbus met the Taino, the native peoples of the island, and was interested in the gold ornaments that they wore suspended from their noses. Using sign language, the natives told Columbus that the gold came from islands that lay to the west and south. Columbus sailed to many islands of the Bahamas, looking for the source of the natives' gold. As they began to better understand one another, Columbus learned from the natives of an island that they called Colba, known today as Cuba. When Columbus arrived in Cuba, he thought he was on a **peninsula** of the Asian mainland because of its large size.

(left and below) Gold was not found in Cuba, but Columbus discovered new foods, such as sweet potatoes, kidney beans, and maize, or corn. They also learned that cotton was grown in the mountains.

- **August 3, 1492** - **Columbus' ships, the** *Nina*, **the** *Pinta*, **and the** *Santa Maria*, **leave Spain.**

- **October 12, 1492** - **Land is sighted.**

- **October 28, 1942** - **Columbus reaches Cuba.**

- **March 14, 1493** - **Columbus returns to Spain, completing his first voyage.**

La Isla Hispaniola

Sailing westward, the *Santa Maria* and the *Nina* reached the harbor of a large island, which Columbus named La Isla Hispaniola, or "the Spanish island." Today this island is known as Hispaniola, and is divided into two countries, the Dominican Republic and Haiti. The natives wore jewelry made from gold, which they said came from Cibao, a region of the island.

The Establishment of La Navidad

On December 24, 1492, Christmas Eve, the *Santa Maria* and the *Nina* left the harbor for Cibao. Just before midnight, the *Santa Maria* hit a reef and the hull, or body of the ship, filled with water. Columbus ordered the crew to abandon ship. Columbus, believing that the shipwreck was a sign from God to stay, established a **colony** there. They built a fort from the timbers of the *Santa Maria*, and named it "Villa de la Navidad," meaning "Christmas town."

(background) When they reached shore on the first island of the Bahamas, Columbus planted the Spanish flag in the ground and claimed the land for Spain. He named the land San Salvador. Historians do not know exactly where Columbus first landed. At one time many believed that he landed on Watling Island, which is present-day San Salvador, in southern Bahamas. Today, it is generally believed that he landed on an island near Samana Cay in the Bahamas.

Homeward Bound

Columbus left 39 men at La Navidad with instructions to explore the area to find a suitable area for settlement, and to trade with the natives for gold. The men were left with food, the *Santa Maria's* boat, and some cannons to defend the fort. Columbus was now certain that he had found Asia, and had enough gold trinkets to convince Queen Isabella and King Ferdinand of his discovery. Columbus left the fort and sailed back to Spain in the *Nina*.

Return to Spain

Columbus met King Ferdinand and Queen Isabella in Barcelona, Spain, where he presented them with gold molded into masks and ornaments, spices, parrots, pineapple, and captured natives. The King and Queen were pleased with Columbus' discoveries, and named him Admiral of the Sea.

Life at Sea

It was difficult to find men to join Columbus' first expedition because many sailors feared shipwrecks, pirate raids, and storms. Most of the men who volunteered were experienced sailors who were seeking money and glory. A few were criminals who joined because they were promised that their crimes would be cleared if they did.

Columbus' Fleet

Columbus had three ships on his first voyage: the *Nina*, the *Pinta*, and the *Santa Maria*. The *Nina* and the *Pinta* were caravels, or fast, lightweight sailing crafts. The caravels were equipped with lateen, or triangular, sails, which enabled them to sail into the wind. The small size of the caravel made it easy to navigate in shallow water. Columbus' **flagship**, the *Santa Maria*, was a large carrack with square sails. Carracks were designed for hauling cargo, and were not normally used for exploration because their large size made them slower and more difficult to maneuver. Cargo, which included food, water, glass beads and bells for trade, and weapons, such as cannons, spears, and crossbows, were stored below deck.

(background) Queen Isabella and King Ferdinand arranged for the carpenters, sail makers, and merchants of Spain to inspect and make necessary repairs to the ships. Columbus carried with him official letters of greeting from Spain to the Great Khan, the emperor of China.

Duties of the Crew

- Captain -

The captain supervised the work of the crew, and determined the course and speed of the ship.

- Pilot -
The pilot navigated the ship.

- Helmsman -
The helmsman steered the ship by moving the rudder.

- Surgeon -
The surgeon cared for sick and injured sailors.

Hardships

The sailors aboard ship were unable to bathe or wash regularly, and lice and fleas were everywhere. Captains, officers, and pilots were the only people who had their own sleeping quarters. The sailors slept on deck where they had to tie themselves down to prevent being tossed into the sea. In bad weather, they went to the hold, the area below deck, to find a dry place to sleep among the food. Many sailors died from illnesses such as scurvy, which was a common disease caused by a lack of vitamin C found in fresh fruit and vegetables. Most of their food, such as meat, was salted or dried so it would not spoil. The crew only ate one meal a day. They ate with their hands and often shared bowls.

Ship Biscuits

Ship biscuits, or hardtack, did not spoil easily and sopped up juices from stews.

(below) The main foods that sailors ate were pickled or salted meats, sardines, olives, peas, cheese, and raisins.

What you need:
2 cups (500 mL) flour
1/2 tsp (5 mL) salt
Water

What to do:
1. Mix the flour and salt, adding water one drop at a time until the dough becomes stiff.
2. Roll out the dough on a board sprinkled with flour. The thickness of the dough should be about 1/3 inch (8 mm). With a knife, carefully cut the dough into squares or circles.
3. Prick the tops of the biscuits with a fork. Bake in an oven at 375°F (190°C) until lightly brown.

Navigation Equipment

Dead reckoning was a navigation technique Columbus used to cross the ocean. The position of the ship was calculated by measuring the course and distance sailed from a known point. Distance was calculated by multiplying the ship's speed by the length of time it had been sailing. A compass was used to determine the course, or direction in which a ship was sailing by reading a needle that pointed to the **magnetic north**. Columbus was also a master at navigating by reading signs from nature, such as the behavior of birds, the color of the sky, and the condition of the seas.

(background) Celestial navigation is a process of calculating the location of the ship by observing the position of the moon and stars.

(right) Another navigational device used was a quadrant, through which a navigator looked at the stars to measure latitude from a string that hung from the top.

- Crew -
The crew worked the sails and pumped the water that collected at the bottom of the ship.

- Ship's boy -
Ship's boys led the morning and evening prayers, scrubbed the decks, and cooked hot meals for the sailors. They were also responsible for keeping track of time, using a sand glass, and singing songs to announce the hour of the day.

Other Voyages

The king and queen of Spain paid for three more of Columbus' voyages. Columbus was instructed to further explore Cuba and to bring more riches back to Spain, and also to discover a sea route to the Asian mainland.

A Second Voyage

Seventeen ships with about 1,500 men, including Columbus' brother, Diego, went on the second voyage. After three weeks of sailing, Columbus planted the Spanish flag on three islands of the **West Indies**. He named the islands Dominica, Mariagalante, after his ship, and Guadeloupe. While in Guadeloupe, he saw new animals, such as geese and parrots, and tasted pineapple for the first time. Columbus sailed across the Caribbean Sea along the coast of Puerto Rico to reach Hispaniola. He passed through many islands of a group called the Lesser Antilles, such as Martinique, St. Lucia, and Grenada. He stopped to explore some of these islands.

Return to Spain

Columbus returned to Spain and presented the king and queen with gold nuggets and Taino slaves. He asked to be outfitted for a third voyage.

Meanwhile, word had reached Spain that the English and Portuguese kings were also preparing to find new sea routes to Asia. Spain wanted to keep these **rivals** out of Hispaniola, so King Ferdinand and Queen Isabella granted Columbus his third voyage.

The Third Voyage

Columbus left Spain with a fleet of six ships, three of them laden with supplies for Hispaniola. He set sail along a southerly course across the Atlantic Ocean to the Cape Verde Islands, then headed northeast until he reached an island in the West Indies that Columbus named Trinidad.

Newfound Hope

Columbus crossed a gulf and sailed through a tidal wave. He named the area *La Boca de la Sierpe*, meaning "the serpent's mouth," which today is known as the Gulf of Paria. Across the gulf, he saw the mountains of the Paria Peninsula on the South American continent, and steering north, he reached the shore of present-day Venezuela.

The High Voyage

Columbus called his fourth and last voyage "el alto viaje," meaning "the high voyage," because he had high hope that this voyage would result in the discovery of the sea route to Asia. Columbus set sail from Cadiz, Spain, with four ships and about 140 men. He crossed the Atlantic Ocean and sailed southwest across the West Indies to search for a westward passage to Asia. He explored the coastline of present-day Honduras, Nicaragua, Costa Rica, and Panama. While sailing to Hispaniola, Columbus ran into a hurricane which battered his ships. His fleet became stranded at a small bay on Jamaica's north coast, where the crew remained for a year.

(background) On Jamaica they survived by using their ships for shelter and trading with the Indians for cassava bread, fish, and corn.

- September 25, 1493 -
Start of second voyage.

- May 5, 1494 -
Columbus reaches Jamaica.

- June 11, 1496 -
End of second voyage. Columbus returns to Spain.

- May 30, 1498 -
Third voyage begins.

- May 10, 1502 -
Columbus embarks on his fourth voyage.

Failed Colonies

Part of the reason that the king and queen sponsored more of Columbus' voyages to the New World was to establish a trading colony there. The land's valuable resources, such as gold, could be shipped back to Spain to increase the country's prosperity.

La Navidad

The first European settlement was the Spanish fort La Navidad, where Columbus left part of his crew on his first voyage. When he returned on his second voyage, he found his crew were all dead. Columbus learned from the Taino that while he had been away, his crew mistreated the natives and demanded from them more gold than they were able to give. In revenge, the Taino destroyed La Navidad and killed the Spaniards.

(above) Fed up with their treatment by the Spaniards, the Taino killed them at La Navidad.

Starting a Colony

Many settlers joined Columbus' fleet on his second voyage, eager to begin a new life in the New World. They did not know that the crew Columbus left behind in La Navidad had all been killed. The settler colonists on the second voyage were craftsmen, farmers, and laborers. They intended to clear the land and build houses, churches, and storehouses for the colony. Columbus' ships carried tools, seeds for planting, and animals such as chickens, cattle, donkeys, sheep, goats, and pigs.

A Failed Colony

A short distance east of La Navidad, in what is now the Dominican Republic, Columbus chose a new site to build a colony, which he named Isabella for the Queen of Spain. When Columbus left the colony at Isabella to explore Cuba, he left his brother, Diego, in command. In his absence, some of the men mutinied, stole ships, and sailed back to Spain, where they told the king and queen that Columbus was a poor **governor**, and that there was no gold.

Santo Domingo

Another of Columbus' brothers, Bartholomew, established a colony at Santo Domingo. The site of the colony was located near a navigable river with easy access to the ocean. The land was fertile and the harbor was sheltered. When Columbus arrived at Santo Domingo on his third voyage, he found that many settlers had died from illness. The settlers disliked taking orders from Columbus and his brothers, and some had befriended natives who had agreed to help them in a rebellion against Columbus.

(right) Some settlements failed and were founded again before becoming permanent.

Banned from the Colony

The Spanish king and queen received many negative reports of the colonies and sent a man named Francisco de Bobadilla to investigate. Bobadilla imprisoned Columbus and his brothers, and sent them back to Spain in chains. Eventually, Columbus' rights to a portion of the New World riches were restored, but the king and queen appointed a new governor to rule the islands. Columbus was ordered to search for gold, silver, gemstones, and spices, but was forbidden from returning to the colony in Hispaniola to avoid further conflict.

Native Life

Columbus and his crew met two groups of natives: the Taino and the Carib. Historians believe that these groups came to the islands from present-day Venezuela. The Taino migrated to the islands of the Greater Antilles around 900 B.C., and the Carib settled into the Lesser Antilles around 1000 B.C.

(background) In Carib villages, houses were built of wooden frames covered with leaves, reeds, and straw and had floors made of packed mud.

Taino Village Life

Native leaders lived in rectangular huts located in the center of the villages. Villages had large plazas, or courts, where members of the community gathered to participate in archery contests, wrestling matches, and dancing. The Taino slept in hammocks made from cotton cloth or string, and ate foods such as potatoes and cassava in bowls made of clay or wood.

The Taino

The Taino lived on the islands of Cuba, Jamaica, Hispaniola, and Puerto Rico. They were skilled hunters, and made dugout canoes for fishing, transportation, and exploring the coast.

The Carib

The Carib settled on the islands of the Lesser Antilles, which included Guadeloupe, Martinique, Dominica, St. Lucia, St. Vincent, Grenada, and Trinidad and Tobago. The Carib were expert navigators who built canoes equipped with sails so they could raid other islands. They attacked the Taino villages with bows and arrows that had poisoned tips, and took the Taino as slaves.

European Contact

The Taino and the Carib were enemies because the Carib had forced the Taino off their lands hundreds of years before. Both groups soon found a new enemy in the Spanish.

Conquering the Taino

Before the Spaniards arrived in Hispaniola, there were about one million Taino living on the island. Most of Columbus' crew believed that the natives' culture and customs were primitive, or backward. The Spanish abused the Taino and Carib. The Spanish bribed the Taino to pan for gold, build settlements, and work in mines by promising them protection from the Carib, as well as food, shelter, and wages. Instead, the Taino did not receive anything for their labor, and many were forced into slavery.

Contact with the Carib

Unlike the Taino, the Carib did not peacefully welcome Columbus and his crew when they arrived on their islands. The Carib were angry to find intruders on their land. During Columbus' second voyage the fleet reached a large island, which Columbus named Santa Cruz, meaning "holy cross." Columbus spotted a village on the island, so he anchored in a bay and sent men in the ship's boat to explore it.

They were met by a canoe of Carib, who attacked the Spaniards with bows and poisonous arrows, killing one of them. The Spaniards shot at the Carib and rammed their boat into the canoe. When a group of Carib began to shoot arrows at the Spaniards from shore, Columbus ordered his crew to leave the island.

(above) The Taino were friendly toward the Spanish when they first arrived.

European Christians

Columbus and his crew were Christians. Christians believe in one God and follow the teachings of Jesus Christ, who they believe is God's son. Christianity was the main religion of Europe during the Middle Ages. When explorers found native peoples practicing other religions, they tried to force them to convert, or change their religion, to Christianity.

(above) European artists could not imagine a people who were not like Europeans. They drew the Taino and Carib with European faces but dancing, smoking, and dressed in exotic clothing.

Forced Converts

Columbus was ordered by the Spanish king and queen to convert the natives to Christianity. After the first voyage, Spanish priests sailed with Columbus. Columbus and the priests believed that God wanted all people to be Christian. Many Spaniards had no understanding or **tolerance** for native religions. The natives were forced to abandon their villages and move to towns that were built by the Spanish. After much suffering, many natives agreed to be **baptized**, and those who did not convert were forced into slavery or were killed.

After Columbus

Christopher Columbus failed in his westward search for Asia, but his arrival in the New World inspired the colonization of the continents of North and South America. As a result, the Spanish empire's wealth grew and native civilizations endured centuries of suffering.

What Happened to Columbus?

When Columbus returned to Spain after his fourth voyage, he was very ill and spent months resting at a **monastery** to regain his health. He spent the next year and a half writing letters asking the king and queen to restore his lost titles of admiral and governor of Hispaniola.

Columbus' titles were not returned, but King Ferdinand granted him two percent of all the riches in the Spanish West Indies. Columbus insisted that Cuba was part of the Chinese mainland even as his death drew near. He died believing that he had reached Asia.

(below) Columbus died and was buried in Spain. Historians believe his remains may have been dug up and moved several times to places such as Hispaniola, Cuba, and Italy.

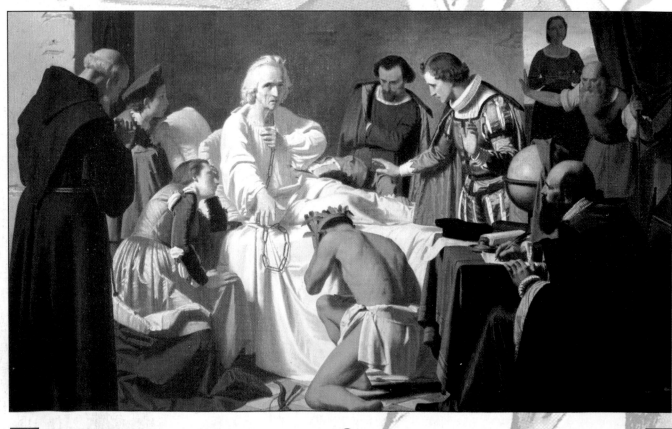

(above) Columbus' brother Bartholomew cruelly destroyed native villages on Hispaniola.

The Conquistadors

After Columbus, Spanish soldiers and explorers, called conquistadors, sailed to the New World to conquer, or take control of, the lands and people living there. The conquistadors waged bloody wars for gold and silver.

Carving up the Land

After Columbus returned to Europe, he wrote a letter to the Pope, the leader of the Catholic Church, to explain what he had found. The Pope issued a papal bull, or announcement, that gave the rulers of Spain control of every island that Columbus discovered. A line was drawn to give land to the west of Cape Verde to Spain, and land to the east to Portugal. Most of South and Central America was colonized by the Spanish.

- 1519 -

Conquistador Hernando Cortes sails to Mexico with 500 men and kills Moctezuma, the Aztec emperor. The Aztec were a powerful native group from what is now Mexico. The Spaniards destroyed Tenochtitlan, the capital city, and claimed the Aztec empire.

- 1532 -
Spanish conquistador Francisco Pizarro and his men battle the Inca at Cajamarca, in what is now Peru. The Inca were a South America native group that controlled a vast empire along the Pacific coast of South America.

(background) *The arrival of the Spaniards in the New World was disastrous for the native population. Historians believe that the Taino became extinct by the end of the 1500s. The deaths of millions of native peoples resulted from slavery, forced labor, starvation, and European diseases that Spanish settlers brought to the islands.*

Future of the West Indies

When the native peoples died from working long hours with little food, slaves were brought from Africa to replace them. In 1510, the first African slaves were brought to the New World on ships. Within a century, about 40,000 African slaves were being brought to the colonies each year. Spain established colonies and trading ports on the islands of the West Indies as new lands were discovered. Pirate ships from England, North Africa, Turkey, and the Netherlands prowled the Spanish trade routes to raid trading ships for valuable cargo, such as gold, trinkets, and food.

How the Americas got their Name

After Columbus failed to discover a westward sea route to Asia, an Italian explorer named Amerigo Vespucci embarked on a voyage to find it. Vespucci sailed from Portugal in 1501, and explored the southern and eastern coasts of South America. Vespucci concluded that the lands were actually new continents, and not part of Asia. His theory was printed in a newspaper called *Mundus Novus* in 1502. A cartographer, or mapmaker, named Martin Waldseemuller read about Vespucci, and believed that he was the true "discoverer" of the Americas. In 1507, Waldseemuller published a map in which he named the New World "America" after Vespucci. He later learned that Columbus was the first European known to reach the New World, but it was too late to correct his error. Everyone in Europe began calling the New World "America."

Columbus' Legacy

More than 500 years have passed since Columbus landed in the Bahamas. Both Europe and the Americas have changed dramatically since then.

New World Influences

Columbus and his crew ate many new foods upon their arrival to the New World. The Taino introduced them to cassava, pineapple, and tobacco. The Taino cultivated several important crops, such as varieties of maize, or corn, potatoes, tomatoes, and squash. Other foods that were grown in the Americas included lima beans, peanuts, cassava, cacao, and pineapple. The natives were also introduced to new foods that the Spanish brought to their islands, such as wheat, rice, coffee, bananas, and olives. Animals such as horses, cows, pigs, and chickens were imported to the New World during the colonization of the islands.

(below) Today there are about 3,000 Carib living in Dominica in the Caribbean. They live on a land reserve that was established in 1903, called the Carib Territory. They are the largest remaining Carib community and continue to practice the Carib culture and language.

Probanzas and the Spanish Conquest

The role of the conquistadors in the Spanish conquest of Central and South America is debated by historians today. The main sources of information about the conquest are first-hand reports written by the conquistadors and their men, which were sent back to the Spanish king. These reports, called probanzas, were written to prove to the king that the conquerors deserved rewards such as titles and pensions for their work.

Some historians today question the facts presented by the conquistadors in these reports, and the role that individuals played in the conquest. The information on events and people in this book are based on the probanzas and some historians' interpretations of these reports.

Artwork

There were no cameras or video recording equipment during the Spanish conquest. The artwork in this book was created later by artists who were not present at the events. For this reason, the events may not have happened exactly as they appear in this book, and are shown in art styles that were popular during the artists' lifetimes.

(right) There are many monuments, towns, and statues named for Columbus. Many people in the United States celebrate Columbus' voyages on Columbus Day, on the second Monday of October every year.

Glossary

astronomer A person who studies and observes the universe beyond Earth, including stars, comets, planets, and galaxies

Bahamas An island country in the Atlantic Ocean

baptize To take part in a religious initiation ceremony to become a Christian

cay A coral reef or sand bar large enough to form a small island

colony Territory that is ruled by another country

course The direction or path that a ship takes

flagship The ship that carries the commander and bears the commander's flag

geographer A person who studies the physical features of the Earth, such as landforms, rivers, and mountains

governor An official who oversees a territory

Latin The language of ancient Rome, which developed into many languages, including French, Italian, and Spanish

magnetic north The direction of the Earth's magnetic pole

mastic The resin, or sap, from a small evergreen shrub

Middle Ages The period in European history from about 500 A.D. to about 1500

monastery A place where monks, or men who have devoted their lives to religion, live

Muslims Followers of Islam. Muslims believe in one god, Allah, and follow the teachings of the prophet Muhammad

mutiny The rebellion of crew members against their captain, often resulting in a takeover of command of a ship

navigate To direct the course, or direction, of a ship

peninsula A piece of land that juts out into a body of water

rivals Competitors

rudder A piece of a ship that is used for steering

sponsor To finance, or pay for, a project or an event carried out by another person or group

tolerance A willingness to accept or understand

trade route A route used by traveling traders or merchant ships

trade winds The winds that blow from the north Atlantic near the equator

Venetian Of or relating to Venice, Italy, or its people, language, or culture

West Indies The islands between southeast North America and northern South America that separate the Caribbean Sea from the Atlantic Ocean. The area is also called the Caribbean

wool carder A person who uses a wire-toothed brush or machine to disentangle wool fibers before spinning

Index

Africa 6, 7, 8, 9, 29
arrest 21
Asia 4, 6-7, 8, 9, 10, 11, 13, 18, 19, 26, 29
Atlantic Ocean 4, 8, 10, 18, 19

Bahamas 5, 11, 12, 30
Bechalla 8
Behaim, Martin 6

Carib 4, 22-23, 24, 25, 30
cassava 23, 30
Christians 25
colony 12, 20-21, 26, 27, 29
Columbus, Bartholomew 21, 27
Columbus Day 30
Columbus, Diego 21
crew 5, 10, 12, 15-16, 17, 18, 20, 24
Cuba 11, 18, 21, 23

da Gama, Vasco 7
death 5, 21, 26, 28
de Bobadilla, Francisco 21
Diaz, Bartolomeu 7
disease 16, 28

early life 4-5, 8

Ferdinand and Isabella 9, 13, 14, 18, 21, 26
first voyage 5, 10-13, 20, 25
fourth voyage 18, 19, 26

gold 11, 12, 13, 20, 21, 24, 27, 29
governor 21, 26
Greater Antilles 22

hammock 23
Henry the Navigator 6
Hispaniola 12, 18, 19, 23, 24, 26, 27

La Navidad 12, 13, 20, 21
Lesser Antilles 18, 22, 23

maize 11, 30
mapmakers 6, 7, 8, 29
Middle Ages 6-7, 25
mutiny 10, 21

navigation 6, 15, 17
Nina 10, 11, 12, 13, 15

pineapple 13, 18, 30
Pinta 10, 11, 14, 15
Pinzon, Martin Alonso 11
Polo, Marco 7
Portugal 6, 8
potato 11, 23, 30
Ptolemy, Claudius 7

Santa Maria 10, 11, 12, 13, 15
San Salvador 12
Santo Domingo 19, 21
second voyage 18, 20, 24
shipwreck 12, 14, 19
slavery 18, 24, 25, 28, 29
South America 19, 26, 27, 28, 29
Spain 4, 9, 10, 11, 12, 13, 15, 18, 19, 27, 19
spices 4, 6, 13

Taino 4, 13, 20, 22-23, 24, 25, 28, 29, 30
third voyage 10, 18-19, 21
Toscanelli, Paolo 7
trade 4, 6, 9, 14

Vespucci, Amerigo 29

weapons 15, 23, 24

1 2 3 4 5 6 7 8 9 0 Printed in the U.S.A. 4 3 2 1 0 9 8 7 6 5